Some Notes on Love

Marco Cavazos

WordRebels.com

Word Rebels Press
506 N. Bishop Ave.
Dallas, TX 75208

Copyright© by Marcos Cavazos, 2020
second edition 2025
All rights reserved.

ISBNs
978-1-7366205-0-2
978-1-7366205-2-6

Library of Congress Control Number:
2021936478
Cover Art by Ivan Reyes
@ivan_reyese

Printed in
United States of America

Some Notes on Love

Sing

Sing as far as your voice will go
I'll listen and wait for the rocks
to crumble

I'll find you where nothing exists

When you can't sing, just listen

I'll shout as far as I can see,
with little hands cupped around
my mouth, but I'll save the singing
for you, and for my listening

It's the best I can offer

We'll meet when nothing exists
When life isn't there to distract us
                              anymore
When life isn't here to fill our ears
with mortal sounds, and petty aches

So sing as far as you can and when your
voice tires, listen for my shouts

Mornings

Mornings, when we blur away our sleep
to see it's all still real.
These little, pretty dreams drip away
with cold water in our crusty eyes.
Look at the mirror. I'm old.
Look at the mirror. I'm old.

It's all still real.

But the dream was so nice,
and I can still feel your breath
and I can still hear your voice.

a dog barks
that goes away too

Now it's just my voice
in my ears   in my head

in that old face in that old mirror.

Shower

God has no use for atheists
but at least the feeling is mutual

He gets you most with love
GGM called it inevitable
                          the scent of bitter almonds
So you fall in love, stay in love, go crazy in love
but
She doesn't love you
or   she's a thousand miles away
or   she lives in the next room
and you buy her groceries, cook sometimes, heat up
the car when it's cold

and
She doesn't love you   well.... not like
that
but sometimes she wears little blue shorts
and it's just enough to make for an interesting
shower

then you go to sleep in your own private room
you wonder what she's thinking about
and
                      It's not you.

Jonny Ashed his Cigarette

Jonny ashed his cigarette
into the street, and
a little girl said:
I saw what you did.

A hundred. A thousand
images flashed in his eyes
What did I do?

She pointed to the flakes
of burnt tobacco scrap.
That.
I saw what you did.

Jonny stared at the flakes.
Fragile. Crumbled. Dead.
Colorless.
Odored only by faded
reminiscence
of inhaled and exhaled
anxiety.

The last wafts of steam
or smoke— a small soul
floating away
to miserable and immemorial
nothingness.

You're right, Jonny said,
I did that.

Snore

She sleeps
with a little puffing
snore— too innocent
for her waking mischief
and very confusing

you freeze when she glances
with blinking (batting) eyes
that say "protect me"
but that's the trick
old man, you're
the one who should run.

Suicide

Suicide
on a Saturday
sounds shocking
enough.

But, I guess
I should leave it be—
I've got more
books

to write out…
a ton more shit to say.
And, it's true,
friends:

I just plain
like myself too much
to be too
dead.

Bogota, 2019

Employment

She took a domestic job
for room & board
in an ugly city.

The man of the house
was fair. Polite,
but cold. Always
kept his distance.

The kids favored her
to the babysitter.
She did the cooking.
Her room was always
cold.

On Saturdays in the Night

On Saturdays in the night, the moon looks brighter
like people are dancing. Singing George and drinking
a local beer.

So we do it here. The singing. Dancing. Drinking.
Local beer. If the moon people see the glow
they wonder if it's people like them.
But the moon's too far away. They say there's no water
and we can't check too often to find the party.
It's expensive. Really far. They say you need
special suits. Bottled Oxygen.

I heard about a man who made it there. A real estate
investor with heavy disposable income.
I told him how I'd been to Latin America, Europe.
Asia. I told him about the food and the bars and the
cafes.

"Sounds like the place I went," he said. "And just
as quiet."

Circles

The world spun in circles
out of frustration.
Out of frustration, she
stopped spinning one day.

We looked around at each other.
Say, human, what's all this?
We looked around at each other
confused in that split second
just before she flung us
to oblivion.

They tried to warn us.
They tried to warn us.
We looked around at each other
in outer space.
We talked about stocks
and toilet paper.

No, it's bigger than that.
She kicked us out.
She'd had enough
of life on Earth.

Where to Next

I drove around till there
was nowhere left to go
and when I got there
I was disappointed.

The whole world is just
one big ball with the same
thing in every direction.
The clock keeps ticking
as slow as she will:
I'm stuck waiting.

Moon

When the sun burns out
light your path
with my love.
The lonely moon
will watch us stroll.

In Mexico City I Bought Camote
(roasted over scrap wood)

In Mexico City, I bought camote
(roasted over scrap construction wood)
I propped against a cement pole
in front of a gasolinera.

The young people flirted
(lounging in their own nooks)
over shared camote or plantain
drizzled with sweetened condensed milk.
Laughs, smiles, taunts, and the screaming
whistle of the camote cart.
Car horns. Police whistles. Barkers
and barking dogs. Cigarettes and cigarette
vendors. Five pesos for a single.

I blinked from the lights. My ears rang.
"How do you make it whistle?" I asked.
"The flute?" He turned a valve.
It screamed. I lounged back again.
I ate my portion of a camote meant for two.

Mexico City, 2019

Thursday Morning Coffee

The metal stools made uncomfortable seating
but they fit with the little n-shaped cement tables.
I'm an advocate for writing in places that overlook
parks, gardens, busy streets… in this case
a skatepark-garden combo.

Double espresso, a mint chocolate, puff a small cigar.
Trying to work on a novel, but distracted
by the skaters and the pondering of when I got fat.
"Hey kid, let me try."
Nah. Better not. I'll break something
that'll take too long to heal.

Another double espresso, this one cold— hipsters
don't run the coffee to the outside tables.
Matter of principle. Added risk of catching cancer
from seeing rolled up tobaxxxo. Minimum: PTSD.
This coffee shop sells mezcal. Well, damn.

Tomorrow's a better day for writing.

Clear growler. Worm salt. Olives? That's new.
Give me nine. Stop bringing new glasses.
Just refill this one.

I'll drop some tacos in the street later,
wake up in the apartment around midnight.
Who left the sparkling water by the bed?
Did I spend, lose, or get robbed of my pesos?

Mexico City, 2019

Maybe Tomorrow

Maybe tomorrow I'll write a poem
or think about you a little less.
Though now I'd rather not
do anything at all.

So I'll lay in bed and count
seconds, trying not to count
while I wait for tomorrow
when I'll get something done
when I'll stop thinking
about you.

Untitled

1.

From your gentle lips
give me your gentle lies
          darling.
Lie with me, us together
through blistering sunlight
over boiling rocks
in a desert as dry
as your tears
     for me.

Whisper, whisper everything
over the deafening roar
of oceanic storms.
I'll pretend to hear Your words
we'll pretend to hold Our bodies
You pretend to love
          darling.

My angel
lie away your sins.
I'll say yes
    darling.

When the ocean waves
crash.
Smile while I drown.
I'll wave to you
from the tossing water
and the gentle flow
of gentle lies.

2.

From your gentle hands
give me your gentle touch
        darling.
I'll feel the softness
of your porcelain flesh
and tell you
        this is true.
And say yes to me
        darling.
Through the frigid wind
over shattered glass
in barren winter landscape
as silent as my words
        for you.

Scream to me, scream for me
darling.
Over the blinding silence
of solid rivers.
In the echo of your sound
I'll pretend to feel your pain.
We'll pretend to see our souls
wrapped together
above the crystal shards

My perfect flower
close your eyes
listen to my lies.

And when the river breaks
free
Smile while you drift.
I'll fasten my wool,

And tell myself
You are warm too.

In Her Bed

"I'm worried about you,"
I sipped a beer.
"Oh?" She smiled, took a drag.
"Yeah." Another sip. "We're
sexually compatible..."
"And?" she turned.
"There must be something
really wrong with you."

Love on Fire

Your love is a forest
I am a fire.
Careless, wreckless
and ravenous
    I eat everything.

Every twig, every
blade of soft grass.

Your trees fall.
Your streams boil away.
Little animals scurry
burning to death.

I flicker over soot
and steam, and a smoke
too dense to live by.

There's nothing left.

Why did you stop
loving me? I ask.

Quiet Tree on a Still Day

When the leaves still
under stale wind
caring not to breeze,
I remember your breath
brushing softly
but speaking loudly
about love
then loss.

In those same moments,
do the leaves mourn
for tranquil gusts?
Once spoiled in continuity,
do they now droop confused?
Or did they forget
there ever existed
the touch of wind?

Old Tree

A fine tree. A hundred years old, or maybe more.
Maybe older, maybe finer than any of us knew.

A chunk of root poked out of the grass
in the shape of a chair. I cradled there
and read books in mild weather.
A fine tree.

I read Kafka. An old man, gray beard said:
You're in my chair. He held a book of Kafka.
Take the chair old man, take the chair.
She's older than both of us.

One day, he said, through one eye, one day
it'll be your turn to be the old man
that kicks the young man out of your chair.

He winked. I smiled. I stood, and my
back popped. I went to the bench,
and read Kafka.

Apartment Plants

I watched her dancing
watering plants.
Little shorts &
flowing translucent
white top, sleeves.

Yellow rays through
the open window
coating each soft
green leaf, some
hanging from open
drawers.

The view from blue
blankets, scented
of lavender.
A quiet Sunday
in a little bedroom.

Hardwood floors
white walls, art
in white frames.
and

the peace of Sunday
so vibrant & perfect.
then
My eyes open to gray
the images fade
with each blink
and breath of frost.
It's cold. It's dreary.
I'm alone.

but what a nice dream it all was.

Broken

He found her searching
in a broken place
confused

This is my space   he said
My broken place

Why do I find you here?

The Between

I thought about you in cold rain because it stung
my skin. I could see your touch in the crystal
sparks. I felt your voice in the wind's hum, so
I closed my eyes to imagine your existence with me.

In that dream, you felt my hand with a shock
that warmed the little bones in my fingers.
When you began to blur, and it all began to end,
I knew it was time to close my eyes.
In the haze of sleeplessness you spoke

      Where are you going?
I want to sleep darling
   The dream just started, you should stay.

It's been two years since my last nap, and I feel heavy
    If you sleep now, when will I see you?

I'll stay another day, darling. But just one more.
  That's all I ask of you. She smiled she
smiled.

I blinked to shake the haze away. I sat up. Cold, but
no rain. "I must've imagined the rain," I said to no
one.

Dizzy

Her smiles turn me
useless, drunk…..
and desperate
for the next one.

So, what's left
but to stumble around
disoriented, confused
and cloudy
for a few days
searching for—
starving for
a distraction.

The kind you find
in bottle, book, or boxing
to leave yourself dizzy
dizzy & forgetful.
so nothing seems
missing.

but it's still missing
that smile
that life
that little way
she bats her eyes
and leaves you the helpless
wanderer waiting
for that little smile.

Between Us

There's a world between
us, and planes aren't flying
but I'll see you soon, babe.
it's only time.

There's plenty to go around.
And if I don't have much,
I'll spend what I have
on waiting for you.

Gin

She swirled the cocktail
     gin
with the olive pick
        steel
and tasted lemons
           salt
bitterness & herbed
           remorse
visions of old relatives
             the dead
and that cutting longing
               memories
desire for forgotten
                 nostalgia
who violates her sleeping
              tranquility
and her dreams about
             the dead
          scattered
        ashes
     discarded for the living.

Natalie

Was it Saturday?
I knew you when
we were young.
Little, feeble, friendly.
Hissing wind hissed
  by our ears.
We brushed our hands
    over wheat
or was it cotton?

My father
  rode a motorcycle.
You waited for a turn
or did I?
And the canal flooded
the wheat field.

Grandfather, a shovel.
I saw that it was
        mud.
"Run," you said.
"Run through the mud."

Love

Take my hand
leap with me
above
broken dreams
piercing memories

inhale

taste our triumph
over
bruised promises
secret truths
hidden monsters

In the depths of your
slumber
sway into my caress

inhale

my beating heart
touch it
but with delicate
grasp
it is yours
love.

Mosquitos

I hear your voice
over the buzz of mosquitos
and we swatted and chatted
drinking cheap rum
and cheap beer
while the hammock rocked
and howler monkeys roared
like hungry lions.
Your eyes were
like lions too.
then you said, "let's fuck."
but we had no water
so we counted money
to plan a different life.

Spinning

Remember how we kissed.
Kissed until the world
stopped spinning.
You laughed
and said
did you feel that?
That sinking?

Remember how we laughed.
I said yeah. What's that
all about?

You shrugged
and said
worry later.
worry later.

Sundays Taste Strange

Sundays still taste strange
when I think about you
and the way you ate your fruit.

Life is always strange in those ways
the funny little things we end up missing
but not understanding why.

It was the smell.
That's what leaves me to think about you.

The mornings sound so much quieter too
when you're not there eating your fruit too loud
making the apartment smell like a fruteria
on a hot day

because you were too cold to crack a window
and the sun shone straight in, making everything
rot in the bowls you left all over the place.

Now it's clean, and it smells clean
and it smells empty.

Anything at All

You could have been anything
but you were born poor.
You were born from a little
neighborhood called
The Cut
and you ate beans
tortillas and bread
and jumped under cars
when they started shooting.

You were born a bastard.
Your dad left for a better family
(at least a more fun one).
They ate good meals
had nice things
never hid under cars,
                    so you heard.

You could have been anything
but your Mom was a drunk
and no one knows
and no one noticed

when you poured liquor
in your milk from 9
years old

when you tried to hang
yourself at 12 or 13.

when you found god
then lost him at 15.

when you wanted to fight
everyone and anything.

when you wrote a book
about war before you
went to war
saw what it was
burned it.

burned your flag too.

You could have been anything
when your mom cleaned up
and you went to college
did alright at that
until you rejected school
G.I. bills, structured education
you called brainwashing.
You dropped out,
drinking again.

You read books that
you stole from corporate
stores, and you disrupted class
embarrassed teachers
in your head, all over again
like when you were a kid.

You lived alone
in a dirty neighborhood
called nothing special
it was between neighborhoods
with names, existed only
for invisible people.

You drank all night
sometimes you didn't get home
or maybe you made it to the front lawn
where a neighbor would wake you
or empty your pockets.

You could have been anything
when they asked: are you okay?
and you said, "sure."
but you weren't sure

and you held the gun
and you held the bottle
you tasted pennies
cheap spirits

imagined your brains
all over the walls

imagined your liver
turning white or yellow

imagined your casket in a hole
your face in a ditch
hospital bed, hospice
the endless clicking
         of a TV remote control
until the channels all lost signal
and you lost signal too

but they wheeled you out
for sunlight and fresh air
while you tried to remember
what was it
that thing that tasted
like pennies.

Lost at Sea

We float:
with changing tides
       and tired eyes.
Will you stop to take
my embrace?
Wake from your trance.
We will dance.
Adrift, lost, indifferent.
Gulps of water...
   and the bite of salt.
Like lonely logs, one wrapped
in silk— your translucent gown.
Stay with me in this abyss.

Lost at sea:
My heart needs only you.
So lay with me, love.
Feel the chill that pangs
the stomach. Take my hand.

You and I, love,
can drift together
through this lonely world
and know:
we only needed us.

Roof Garden

Car horns all night & lights too
from who knows where.
She smoked her cigarette
on the roof garden hammock
with a leg dangled off the edge.

I wondered about conversation
trying to remember words
here or there all combined
to say something interesting
in her language.

Elevator ding, some dude
with a lot more words
that sound good for smoking to
not to mention cold bubbles.
So back to ink and paper
to work on poems.

Or maybe to my room & books
that I can flip through a while
pretend to read then put on porn
      with no volume— there's neighbors.

Bored of that too. More horns, lights,
the god damned mosquitos
that never go away.
So back to that roof garden

to see what happened
with the bubbles guy
who knows all the Spanish.

Turns out she speaks German.
Turns out everyone is lonely.

Drinking About You

I gave you my soul.
"I like it," you said
but it was too heavy
and from the burden
        you drowned.

Water Birds

Think of the wind.
Is it cold now?
Remember
when it was warm
and water birds mixed
with crashing waves
and you rocked
in the hammock.
"I don't want to go back,"
you would have said.
"Then stay," he'd say,
as he'd smoke my cigar.

Rocks

the moon needs the sun
to be beautiful.
one time we landed a craft
there and found out it was dead.

We brought back some rocks
before the Russians could.
                    Victory.

Phone Calls

I'd hoped she'd called today.
But the phone never rang.

The damn thing never rang.
I'd hoped she'd called today,
then I'd hoped anyone had
called.

In the morning, I'll look.
Maybe she'd called. Maybe
anyone had called.

Mop

She sways her mop
and it looks
like dancing

I think:
How nice to be the mop.

He Slept on His Side of the Bed

Something like eleven years,
he slept on his side of the bed.
Waiting for her to come back.
She never did.

But he straightened the sheets
arranged pillows.
His arm hung off the edge.
He rolled when it numbed,
but he never moved
to the middle, nor bothered
her side of the bed.

Love is Alone in Bed

He's on another one
she thought, alone in bed,
wondering: will he come home?
He'd always came home.
But always is only always
until it's not.

She finished a lukewarm tea,
read the same line over
and over from the same page.
After a few cigarettes,
the room felt clammy,
so she opened a window, and
tried not to check the time.

Love is alone in bed,
she thought, alone & waiting.
Come morning, she brewed coffee,
cleaned two mugs from a pile
of dirty dishes in a dirty sink.
She went back to bed
to sleep for an hour or two,
forgetting the coffee
and the clean mugs.

Back Home

There's only cigarettes
in that dirty ashtray.
One after another
in an empty chair
in an empty body
while the TV hums.

His eyes hurt
his head hurts.
He eats his meals there
in that chair
off a pressed wood, folding
TV dinner caddy—
food hot from the microwave.

This is how he lives now.
This is how he lives
everyday.

While everyday
under the hum
behind the colors
they die in his head
on repeat.

Clothes Line

Wet clothes, half frozen
hang off the droopy line
under a sturdy tree.

Nothing to wear
it's all half frozen
but Tía insists
on washing.

So we wear
the same clothes
back to back
and all pretend
we haven't noticed
she's losing it.

Across the tree,
on the shade side,
a chunk of limestone
marks where
we buried the dog
named after Grandma.

He had been old,
hadn't been himself.
"He's losing it," we'd say.

Absinthe, Again

I fell for her
before she ever knew
I existed.
Stolen glances
from the bar.
Absinthe drip numb.

She pulled me
into an elevator
        closet.
One of those tiny
rebellions that make
dangerous people
from innocent things.
Well, innocent enough.

Lakeview

I go to the lake to drink about you
and to touch the cool water
and ponder life

the one we promised
the one we made
then & now & when

the swoosh… and that lapping
like a dog at the bowl
and the algae air…
This is real. And this is all.

So I wait in my little room
while I dwell on purpose & meaning
and the trash man comes on Thursday.
I wheel down the bin
one day they'll wheel me off too.

I Dreamed She Rode a Motorcycle

Arms clenching his biker
leather, Mexico City smog
soaking through her pores.
They laughed, smiled.
Free. In a pretend love
in a pretend life.

I woke up.
The dream was over,
and she came home.

Her dream was over too.
Everything was over.
Just dirty clothes & real life.

Poem

You
in that yellow dress.
Jesus.

Untitled

I wanted to love you
but you never gave me
                the chance.
Except to say I love you
with arms closed and eyes shut
never opening your heart
to feel love or be loved.

Just the doubts and the words
and promises behind walls.
Here I am. Here I was.
Love wastes to water
forgotten in the streams.
Feel the words. Feel the sound.
It's all quiet now.

Bodies

Sleep, love
in my arms, close your eyes
dream of us. An existence
absent our bodies.
Our souls entwined—
suspended from living
to love without constraints
of time or space.
There— we can love.
This, love, is too
strong for something
so little as living.

Wanderlust

They went looking
for someone to love
found a bunch
of airline tickets
traveler's diarrea
and one night stands.

Gray Suit

They buried him in a gray suit.
Custom made, Italian fabric.
They put him in a high-end box, too.
Everything else, he left behind.
But the watch, he took the watch.

"What a great man, he owned
so many things," they said.

The kids stepped up for their turn
to collect paper status
to acquire shiny things
to exploit land and labor
to sell their wealth and souls
so someone would say

they were great, they owned
so many things.

Avenues

We trampled lonely
avenues
all over Latin America
but none of it mattered.

Trying to lose our lost
forget our fucks given.
To try again, that
distractions small or
large may sometimes cure

though rarely do
and seldom dealt
to tranquil resolution.

But nightmares fade
to fuzzy gray,
assumed we healed, but
only still running away.

Mexico City, 2019

Hours

He'd sit in his chair for hours
dreaming about the world.
What it all meant.   He did this for years;
                                  made a book out of it.
                                  So what's it all about?
                                  they asked him.

It means nothing, he said.

                                  We just all want it
                                  to be something more.

Life with Her

She understands life
in a way I dream I could.
So I dream about her.

But that dream is a take, not a give.
I have nothing to give and lots to take.

I think I'd like to live like her, I'd be happy.
But, I'd find a way to make everyone else

miserable.

Nothing New

She stood in the road
with the heart pumping
in her hands.
"Seen that before…"
I said. "Heart in hand."
And the tears flowed.
"Seen that too."

She shrugged,
tucked it in her pocket.
"They all just walk by,"
she said.

"They're late some place."
I walked on. "They've
all seen it, too."

Streetlight

We stared at the moon
watching her glow
but she was only
a streetlight.

Our eyes were hazy,
we both forgot our glasses.
But, we searched the sky
for her.

Fog or trees or night
clouds covered
the real moon.

I guess the streetlight
will do. She's all we have.

Untitled

it only takes
a passing woman
to show a man
how lonely he is

On Laughs & Lies

I laugh a little
        louder
when you're around.
Little ways
       to say
             I'm fine.
You're fine. It's all
                alright.
This.
This confused
           cluster
of self-torment, self-hate...

self.

But keep going

    listen to the laughs

        but only hear the lies.

Some Notes on Love

We played this game
where we were the end
all, be all, for years.
Thousands, a couple
hundred thousand.

When it was over
the world kept on
spinning, forgetting
what humanity was.

We smoked our last
cigarettes. Jotted
some notes on love
for future life.

Then it all got quiet,
and the world kept on
spinning, forgetting
yesterday's million
years.

Trash Day

Her hands wet, she looked out of the kitchen window
towards the squealing. Towards the gray bin.
"They just pick it up," she said.
"Every Thursday."
She scrubbed at a dirty plate.
"Don't even charge for it."

"Mama, can I wear the dress to school?"
"No. Hang it up. It's expensive."
"I want to wear it."
"It's for the service."
"I want to wear it."

The little girl climbed onto the counter
next to the dishes air drying on a blue rack.
"Will lots of people be there?"
"All your dad's friends, baby."

She shook her hands dry.
She watched through the window.
The truck's mechanical arm
lifted the bin, shook it out.
"Every Thursday," she said.
"Don't even charge for it."

Lost in her Yellow Dress

She looked lost
in her little yellow
dress, walking
her little yellow
dog.

He shit on the cement
where everyone walks.

She kept on
in her little yellow
dress, walking
looking like she
wanted to look
lost. Like this
isn't the type
of neighborhood
where she usually
picks up shit.

Fish

Another cast. Still water
the buzz of an insect, the sort
that makes you swat the air.
He stared at the reflections.

The water felt cool, but the sun
stung. It stung
until it went away.

He fished all night
from that last cast, and caught
nothing.

When his knees ached,
he stretched out
laid down in the rough grass,
pinched the rod in his armpit.

The reflections turned to dancers.
"What a strange play," he thought.
"They move so slow."

The crickets chirped their songs
till morning. And in the morning,
he wished it were night again.

The Catch

I've always liked fishing
but I don't care for the catch.

I'd rather sit quietly
with a line in the water
and the demons in my head.

To resolve the heavy issues.
internally. externally.
globally.

if only the damn fish
would leave me alone.

Love Poem

Jesus fucking Christ
I need a drink.

Camphor

He'd never been to Kyoto, but he
saw the photographs she snapped
under the pink blossoms of the
Sakura tree.

He'd close his eyes. He'd try to
imagine being there with her, but
in the confines of his imagination,
he'd instead find himself amongst
the dead monks in Okunion—

sitting below a thousand year old
moss covered Camphor, listening to
bullfrogs and monkeys. Letting the
plops of cold rain wake his skin
under the quiet rays of grave
reflected moonlight.

A light so dim, he felt invisible.
In the cemetery, he felt close
to her.

Clouds

Short clouds— too transparent, too…
to make sense of predicting a storm
or any other excitement.
I could go for a weather ritual…
a rain dance, a human sacrifice
or anything else
          with reasonable potential
for breaking apart the god damned
talk
      about the clouds, the weather.

I'll change the subject to women or war
(there's always a new one somewhere).
Drone on and on— but too dull still
re-evaluating political stances
          about short clouds.
Well, how about some rumors…
"Is it true that guy Nick died?"
Yeah, heart attack… knew him well,
you know… he would have loved
this weather.

some notes on love

Thank you for reading. I hope you enjoyed this collection.

-Marco

Marco Cavazos was born and raised in South Texas. He currently lives in Dallas.

Reach out:

Instagram @RealMarcoCavazos

506 N. Bishop Ave.
Dallas, TX 75208

@PoetsBooks

WordRebels.com
PoetsBooks.com

www.ingramcontent.com/pod-product-compliance
Lightning Source LLC
Chambersburg PA
CBHW052205070526
44585CB00017B/2074